WELCOME TO THE FLORAL WORLD

This book belongs to

....

COLOR TEST

TEST YOUR COLOR SUPPLIES ON THIS PAGE TO SEE HOW THEY REACT TO THE PAPER.

This page is left balnk
intentionally to assist with removal
framing or display and minimize
bleed through.
HOWEVER, feel free to use it and
color it the way you like.

This page is left balnk
intentionally to assist with removal
framing or display and minimize
bleed through.
HOWEVER, feel free to use it and
color it the way you like.

This page is left balnk
intentionally to assist with removal
framing or display and minimize
bleed through.
HOWEVER, feel free to use it and
color it the way you like.

This page is left balnk
intentionally to assist with removal
framing or display and minimize
bleed through.
HOWEVER, feel free to use it and
color it the way you like.

This page is left balnk
intentionally to assist with removal
framing or display and minimize
bleed through.
HOWEVER, feel free to use it and
color it the way you like.

This page is left balnk
intentionally to assist with removal
framing or display and minimize
bleed through.
HOWEVER, feel free to use it and
color it the way you like.

This page is left balnk
intentionally to assist with removal
framing or display and minimize
bleed through.
HOWEVER, feel free to use it and
color it the way you like.

This page is left balnk
intentionally to assist with removal
framing or display and minimize
bleed through.
HOWEVER, feel free to use it and
color it the way you like.

This page is left balnk
intentionally to assist with removal
framing or display and minimize
bleed through.
HOWEVER, feel free to use it and
color it the way you like.

This page is left balnk
intentionally to assist with removal
framing or display and minimize
bleed through.
HOWEVER, feel free to use it and
color it the way you like.

This page is left balnk
intentionally to assist with removal
framing or display and minimize
bleed through.
HOWEVER, feel free to use it and
color it the way you like.

This page is left balnk
intentionally to assist with removal
framing or display and minimize
bleed through.
HOWEVER, feel free to use it and
color it the way you like.

This page is left balnk
intentionally to assist with removal
framing or display and minimize
bleed through.
HOWEVER, feel free to use it and
color it the way you like.

This page is left balnk
intentionally to assist with removal
framing or display and minimize
bleed through.
HOWEVER, feel free to use it and
color it the way you like.

This page is left balnk
intentionally to assist with removal
framing or display and minimize
bleed through.
HOWEVER, feel free to use it and
color it the way you like.

This page is left balnk
intentionally to assist with removal
framing or display and minimize
bleed through.
HOWEVER, feel free to use it and
color it the way you like.

This page is left balnk
intentionally to assist with removal
framing or display and minimize
bleed through.
HOWEVER, feel free to use it and
color it the way you like.

This page is left balnk
intentionally to assist with removal
framing or display and minimize
bleed through.
HOWEVER, feel free to use it and
color it the way you like.

This page is left balnk
intentionally to assist with removal
framing or display and minimize
bleed through.
HOWEVER, feel free to use it and
color it the way you like.

This page is left balnk
intentionally to assist with removal
framing or display and minimize
bleed through.
HOWEVER, feel free to use it and
color it the way you like.

This page is left balnk
intentionally to assist with removal
framing or display and minimize
bleed through.
HOWEVER, feel free to use it and
color it the way you like.

This page is left balnk
intentionally to assist with removal
framing or display and minimize
bleed through.
HOWEVER, feel free to use it and
color it the way you like.

This page is left balnk
intentionally to assist with removal
framing or display and minimize
bleed through.
HOWEVER, feel free to use it and
color it the way you like.

This page is left balnk
intentionally to assist with removal
framing or display and minimize
bleed through.
HOWEVER, feel free to use it and
color it the way you like.

This page is left balnk
intentionally to assist with removal
framing or display and minimize
bleed through.
HOWEVER, feel free to use it and
color it the way you like.

This page is left balnk
intentionally to assist with removal
framing or display and minimize
bleed through.
HOWEVER, feel free to use it and
color it the way you like.

This page is left balnk
intentionally to assist with removal
framing or display and minimize
bleed through.
HOWEVER, feel free to use it and
color it the way you like.

This page is left balnk
intentionally to assist with removal
framing or display and minimize
bleed through.
HOWEVER, feel free to use it and
color it the way you like.

This page is left balnk
intentionally to assist with removal
framing or display and minimize
bleed through.
HOWEVER, feel free to use it and
color it the way you like.

This page is left balnk
intentionally to assist with removal
framing or display and minimize
bleed through.
HOWEVER, feel free to use it and
color it the way you like.

This page is left balnk
intentionally to assist with removal
framing or display and minimize
bleed through.
HOWEVER, feel free to use it and
color it the way you like.

This page is left balnk
intentionally to assist with removal
framing or display and minimize
bleed through.
HOWEVER, feel free to use it and
color it the way you like.

This page is left balnk
intentionally to assist with removal
framing or display and minimize
bleed through.
HOWEVER, feel free to use it and
color it the way you like.

This page is left balnk
intentionally to assist with removal
framing or display and minimize
bleed through.
HOWEVER, feel free to use it and
color it the way you like.

This page is left balnk
intentionally to assist with removal
framing or display and minimize
bleed through.
HOWEVER, feel free to use it and
color it the way you like.

This page is left balnk
intentionally to assist with removal
framing or display and minimize
bleed through.
HOWEVER, feel free to use it and
color it the way you like.

This page is left balnk
intentionally to assist with removal
framing or display and minimize
bleed through.
HOWEVER, feel free to use it and
color it the way you like.

This page is left balnk
intentionally to assist with removal
framing or display and minimize
bleed through.
HOWEVER, feel free to use it and
color it the way you like.

This page is left balnk
intentionally to assist with removal
framing or display and minimize
bleed through.
HOWEVER, feel free to use it and
color it the way you like.

This page is left balnk
intentionally to assist with removal
framing or display and minimize
bleed through.
HOWEVER, feel free to use it and
color it the way you like.

This page is left balnk
intentionally to assist with removal
framing or display and minimize
bleed through.
HOWEVER, feel free to use it and
color it the way you like.

This page is left balnk
intentionally to assist with removal
framing or display and minimize
bleed through.
HOWEVER, feel free to use it and
color it the way you like.

This page is left balnk
intentionally to assist with removal
framing or display and minimize
bleed through.
HOWEVER, feel free to use it and
color it the way you like.

This page is left balnk
intentionally to assist with removal
framing or display and minimize
bleed through.
HOWEVER, feel free to use it and
color it the way you like.

This page is left balnk
intentionally to assist with removal
framing or display and minimize
bleed through.
HOWEVER, feel free to use it and
color it the way you like.

This page is left balnk
intentionally to assist with removal
framing or display and minimize
bleed through.
HOWEVER, feel free to use it and
color it the way you like.

This page is left balnk
intentionally to assist with removal
framing or display and minimize
bleed through.
HOWEVER, feel free to use it and
color it the way you like.

This page is left balnk
intentionally to assist with removal
framing or display and minimize
bleed through.
HOWEVER, feel free to use it and
color it the way you like.

This page is left balnk
intentionally to assist with removal
framing or display and minimize
bleed through.
HOWEVER, feel free to use it and
color it the way you like.

This page is left balnk
intentionally to assist with removal
framing or display and minimize
bleed through.
HOWEVER, feel free to use it and
color it the way you like.

This page is left balnk
intentionally to assist with removal
framing or display and minimize
bleed through.
HOWEVER, feel free to use it and
color it the way you like.

www.ingramcontent.com/pod-product-compliance
Lightning Source LLC
Chambersburg PA
CBHW080221260726
48658CB00008B/2958

9 798741 636480